D1233568

ANIMALS HOUSED IN THE PLEASURE OF FLESH

Animals Housed In The Pleasure Of Flesh

Poems by
George Looney

BLUESTEM PRESS
Emporia State University
Emporia, Kansas

ACKNOWLEDGEMENTS

Poems contained in this volume originally appeared in journals as follows:

The Cincinnati Poetry Review: "Local History"
Connecticut Review: "The Urge to Speak"
Denver Quarterly: "The Inevitable Beauty of Gravity"
Flyway Literary Review: "The Tongues of Water Birds"
Hayden's Ferry Review: "The Etched Shape of the Heron" (under the
    title "The Possibility of Touch")
Kestrel: "Animals Housed in the Pleasure of Flesh"
The Literary Review: "Where Rivers Come Together"
Sonora Review: "Morning Visitation"

Copyright © 1995 by George Looney
Cover Art by James Lowrey
Design by Christopher Howell
Technical Assistance: Cliff Dieker

Library of Congress Cataloging-in-Publication Data

Looney, George, 1959-
    Animals housed in the pleasure of flesh : poems by George
Looney.
        p. cm.
        ISBN 1-878325-15-9 (alk. paper). — ISBN 1-878325-14-0
(pbk. : alk. paper)
        I. Title
PS3562.0597A82   1995
811'.54—dc20   95-25708
                                                            CIP

Bluestem Press books are published by the English Department of
Emporia State University, Emporia, Kansas 66801, and are distributed
by:

Small Press Distribution, 1814 San Pablo Ave., Berkeley, CA 94702

The author wishes to thank the National Endowment for the Arts and
the Ohio Arts Council for their support.

Table of Contents

And I drifted away from them, slow, on the pull of the river,
reluctant, looking back at their roost,
calling them what I'd never called them, what they are,
those dwarfed transfiguring angels,
who flock to the side of the poisoned fox, the mud turtle
crushed on the shoulder of the road,
who pray over the leaf-graves of the anonymous lost,
with mercy enough to consume us all and give us wings.

—*David Bottoms*

And we
        who always think
                of happiness *rising*
would feel the emotion
        that almost startles us
                when a happy thing *falls.*

—*Rainer Maria Rilke*

For Mairi, Douglas, Andrea, and Ellen,
and for my mother

A Catechism on Longing

Any bird might translate the sky into a catechism.
The way this marsh sparrow's body of dusk
might answer the absence that sings in you like a psalm
when you touch the woman whose voice is the scar
of a cardinal's passage. The way the gray nuance of wrens
wrapped around a backyard feeder could answer
the expectation of loss in her scent. All faiths
disguise the response of the flesh to the abstract
sorrow of diminishment. The problem is always
the physical. Promises of pleasure, like tree swallows
skimming the seeded tips of grass in some abandoned field,
must bandage the wound the rest of her life makes in you,
a thin gauze wrapped loose in layers and held together
with some prayer chanted in another tongue. But pleasure
is itself a betrayal of the physical, and no more an answer
than sorrow is a field you'd choose to lie in. Even if
kestrels could be seen strafing their small hawk shadows
over grass like some question of the embodiment of touch
in something as transitory as flesh. There's no answer
for the way the body remembers. What your tongue
teases from the aromatic skin between the shoulder blades
of a woman can't answer this cardinal come again
to the feeder like a shock of the familiar. Pain,
which comes like another language with touch,
wants to answer the heron wading the shallows
of a river lowered by months of drought. But the form
carved out of air by its flight is more than a question
of memory trembling with the actual presence
of flesh. This slow, etched form translates the sky,
with its passion of light, the field, where soil holds
the past like a lover, and the river into a language
where faith is possible and nothing's disguised,
not even the desperate prayer of an embrace.

Where Rivers Come Together

A trick of light, and the strokes in an etching by Dürer
coalesce into the figure of a woman on a porch
with what could almost be a wolf or coyote
beside her, its wind-stroked fur an etching
of dirty ice on a river scorched by blades.

Surfaces teach us of love. The way a snowfall changes
the longing of the land for whatever sky's been emptied.
The way any surface is the result of distance.
As if it weren't us. As if the world were not
what we make it, pulled by dogs down streets so dark
the sound of a river is almost a kind of light.

In the Dürer, light forms the musculature
of Adam's arm as it reaches for the single leaf
on the body of Eve, a body nearly of light, both
bodies fields where light whispers in the grass
named by the touch of light. And desire
is the sound of what could be a river in the dark.
Having heard the Ohio in a woman you've touched,
you want to speak rivers you haven't heard.

The woman on the porch could speak of the *Salzach,*
the *salt river,* which could almost convince you it's not
water, but turquoise you could cut stones from
to give to a woman who on a dare, once balanced
on the rail of a fragile bridge high above the river.
The gulls complained at her being almost of the air.

Pound wanted to gather out of the air a live tradition.
What could be more alive than the river
in a woman? What is the buried tradition of rivers?
In particular, any river of salt which carves

what may be desire in your body, the memory
of a woman who is light, since light names
all bodies of vision, or water, or what it carves.

Dürer's Eve is carved of light. And desire
is what the snake wants to bite into, not the apple,
which is the wrong fruit anyway. Even the fruit
is a lie. Even a dirty river can be turned. Like
the Ohio was turned more than a hundred years ago
by the earth rising along a faultline. Willows
on islands in the river twisted and broke, uprooted
by water moving a new way. The dead of
New Madrid, Illinois slid in, moved by confusion.
All rivers carry off both memory and desire,
the dead one form the desire for memory takes.
Those neglected bodies became silt, like a family
dropped by a bridge collapsing into the *Salzach*
that was forgotten in the salt cursing of water.

Inside a house near the river where a woman
drinking coffee almost saw the bridge collapse,
frescoes of baroque devils whisper of the water
in bodies that carves desire like the lines Dürer made
to form the shadows which shape the delicate flesh
of Eve's hand with the apple. It's not clear
whether Eve means to offer the apple to Adam, the snake,
or to the darkness almost moving behind them
which can only be God. The two figures of light
could be standing on the porch of a house with frescoes
painted by a bruised madman laughing on his back.

It could be snowing, the *Salzach* scarred by the blades
of men whose breath rises from bodies warm
with memory. The snow could almost be burning
in a light from the house or whatever moon is left
like a longing in the sky whispered

by a woman who's been bruised by flesh
and blood devils in a winter ritual when
the anger that etches the dour bodies of men
is acted out, their faces grotesque masks.

Or it could be summer, the river the Ohio.
Light could touch the surface and be mistaken
for desire, or love, or the nearly-forgotten language
Dürer etched words from in an open book
hung over a branch to claim this Adam, this Eve.
Or the gray light of winter could claim a woman
walking a dog by the Ohio and remembering another river
in a landscape Dürer would know the language of.
Her skin could be the light Dürer wanted to claim for Eve,
or the apple. It would be, if not for how the gray
longing of the Ohio sky seems to bruise her body.

The river is not closed off yet by ice, and you are
no ghost, no dead engraver. You want to name a river
after the distant mountain goat Dürer put in
the one place of light in the landscape other than
the bodies of Adam and Eve. You want
to bury your hand in its fur and feel what light can
only imagine, knowing this would be different
from the fur of masks worn by the *Krampusse*,
masks too large to be mistaken for anything human.
In some countries, bruises on women's bodies
in winter could form the goat's name, and fear
is a miracle that pierces the skin of saints. In Ohio,
a woman says what could be a name or its ghost,
her breath rising gray by a half-frozen river.

And desire could be where rivers come together
in a woman, flowing into one another
to form one body both flesh and the memory
of flesh, desire and the light that's a longing

in the bodies Dürer cut out of darkness
which, left untouched, was only a god.
And no god can reconcile the distance
the river in a woman flows, or name the light
on its water, or the form of longing it cuts.

The Tongues of Water Birds

From here to a bird that flies
with its neck folded back to its shoulders
is nothing but air, nothing but first light and summer
and water rising in a smoke of waters.
—Stanley Plumly

It's late. Your lover sleeps in another room.
In another country, burnt soil smolders,
the remains of a ceremony of loss.
Ash you'd chant to and smudge your body with.
The back yard could be a breath you took
years ago and held till nothing was left.
Not even the memory of hands cool
with the discipline of mud under your back,
on your thighs. Nothing that sure.
Even the thought of your own body
is murky, memory a gauze for cuts
made in soil or in bodies. Or both.
And a blue heron fishes the filthy river
on the edge of this fogged-in, blind town
in Ohio. There are blue herons in the fog.
And you're not who you thought you were
going to be. Not the ash. Not the mud.
Admit it. Confession might make it easier
to take. That breath you took years ago
haunts you the way fog clings to the grass
like gauze. Confession might not heal anything.
Physician, you've heard it said, *heal thyself.*

Only so much damage can be healed.
In some tribe on a continent you imagine
a woman lets a priest cut off
her clitoris. Maybe a loon cries out.

Maybe it wants a grace of its own,
and a voice to call down flocks of loons,
their striated bodies dropping from the sky
in revenge or pleasure. You want to know which.
You want to take a breath on a continent
where soil never dries out. You want the breath
of the woman asleep in the next room
to be a river where herons and loons
call with voices that can heal anyone.

You want the loons to be pleasure
that has nothing to do with ash or skin,
loss, or the distance between you
and who you thought you were going to be.
You want the heron to be a confession
of how the woman whose breath formed
this river can't be denied. The heron
is flying, its voice something cut
from your body. From memory.

And the need you have for healing
has nothing to do with loons,
or any wound as distant as a continent
you can't imagine. The breath you hear
is no heron. And the only confession
you have to make is made in your body
against your lover's, how it becomes
a poultice placed like prayer over the body
of a woman who, almost awake, speaks
in the benedictive tongues of water birds.

In Your Baseball dreams

after Richard Hugo

It starts innocently enough. Grass burns in light you believe
isn't real. At first there's only one man, a soiled glove
slipped over his left hand. Or else there's a man and a woman
in the uncut grass of a field you once read a corpse
was discovered in, the head crushed by what the news said
could have been a baseball bat. The woman's shirt drapes
the man's left hand. A wind covers his fingers in cloth
and strokes a thin gauze of pollen around their bodies,
and yours. The woman turns her naked back to the man,
whose hands pull her jeans into the grass. She's on her knees,
touching the man's scrotum, when you remember this
started with a man, a glove, and a ball coming at you
as if you have to do more than just watch in this dream.
And you do. You catch the ball in the glove you always knew
bandaged your left hand. Dust and pollen explode the air
around your eyes. You sneeze. And the woman is lost
in the grass under the man, her voice lifting like an insect
from the almost yellow wild grass. It hasn't rained in weeks,
her back singed by the brittle blades. Like the ones
cutting into your bare feet as you heave the baseball back
to the man who has turned away from you. Before
you can warn him, another man catches the ball.
The sound it makes collapsing into his glove echoes
the distant curse of a bat connecting with a woman's skull
which opened to let the violence slip into the grass,
and through the grass into the soil which you can taste now
as the baseball hits your glove again. Off in the grass
the man is tasting the woman, his tongue trying to
articulate a force in this woman who has pollen
and stiff grass and soil stuck to her back. And the air,
swelling with pollen, blurs at the edges as more men

move their arms in what's become a ritual gesture
in this field where even grass has become a conspiracy
you want to believe isn't a murmur of green, but more
a moan, like the man's tongue finds in the woman's body.
Or the almost white shriek this field becomes dusted with snow.
The way it was the day in February a boy found the body
of a woman with a crevice where her face should have been.
There was snow on what was left of her clothes, but her skin
was still warm enough to turn the crystal lyric of water
back into its more mundane nature. The boy knelt down
to brush the snow from the cloth that wound over the woman
like a shroud and, though he didn't think to do it,
and for twenty years he wouldn't remember, he touched
the cold-raised nipples of the corpse with his tongue.

And it's while the almost white curves of the baseballs make lines
through the pollen of this field in summer that you remember
the bland taste of that quiet flesh. How the cold ridges of
skin seemed a map for a country you couldn't yet name,
but knew you'd fall into some day. The glove on your hand
is wet and beginning to itch. You want to pull it off,
but the sweltering air is as full of baseballs as pollen,
and they're moving so fast the stitches are blurred scars.
You're afraid if one struck your ungloved hand it would break skin
and leave a ragged scar like a letter naming the past.
You're afraid of even the stray thought of one being hit
with a bat. It could open down herringbone seams and release
other bodies lost in the uncut fields of grass gone to seed,
in memory. You see, through a haze of hurled baseballs,
the torso and unmarred head of the woman risen above
the seed-burdened stems of dry grass. The man is buried in
a memory of his own, the woman straddling his prone body
almost replaced by another woman. There are so many
baseballs in the air now no one could count them, and you want to
walk over to the seed-covered woman saying the name
of a man and lick the pollen and sweat from her back.

But the air is off-white and dangerous, and distance is a voice

you imagine is the echo of the last breath of the woman
whose breasts invited you into this dream where you are
paralyzed by the memory and loss thrown by the sore arms
of people who have donned old gloves in the sunlight
visible in the raw drift of pollen. So much grief,
and so much pleasure, has been played out in the subtle
impressions of bodies still barely articulate in this grass
you believe is as innocent as a reservoir, the body
of a woman wavering in its water, luminous
pollen settling on algae the texture of a woman's hair
tangled from turning in her sleep or the crosshatching of grass
matted down by bodies. Of water, you'd like to say
it's a comfort. That if you could reach the public fountain
the water you'd swallow would be cold and uncontaminated
by even the memory of flesh. It would come from
a reservoir surrounded by reedy grass, the kind that hides
most anything. Of innocence, you'd like to say nothing
comes of it. That no matter where anything begins,
it always comes back to blurs in the air that could be baseballs,
or pollen, or something as unreliable as memory.
You can hear Claire Lejeune, in a room where smoke curls
in the rhythm of her voice as though it were a lover
or the calm surface of a body of cold water, saying
The ultimate object of human fear is Beauty. The only way
out of this field of grass that goes on dying, being crushed
into impressions of the bodies of lovers and children playing,
is to accept the fact the past is a gauze that is stitched
to our flesh. And every gesture of longing that does no damage,
even the drift of a boy's tongue on the cool skin
of a reservoir or the body of a woman raped and murdered
and dumped in a field of dead grass whitening
in a late February snow, every gentle touch,
is an act of contrition in the pollen, and a prayer
your body writes to praise what you still call beauty.

The brilliant bodies, scarred and sweaty, of the baseballs

curve past you into other gloves covered with cursive letters
you imagine are drafts of a story someone's still revising,
or perhaps the frantic prayer written after the first death.
The woman and the man have dressed and stand on mowed grass
in the haze of pollen past where baseballs fill the air.
This close, you recognize them and know what's beginning
in her body, the embrace of solid and fluid. You are
beginning. And the woman whose body had floated face down
in the cold water of the reservoir has turned over
and is laughing. *Fooled you,* she says, her almost naked form
convincing you it's time to wake up. To embrace the woman
sleeping beside you, her body a whispered matin for beauty
that can let you ignore the baseballs and forget the pollen
and all its echoes, except the goosepimpled flesh
of the woman who's played a prank and leads you
back to the field of uncut grass where a vague impression
of both your bodies hums with the mating call
of some insect. You remember being afraid of
something, but her body, covered in pollen, is real
enough to confess everything to. And you do.

The Good Suffering Does

Pleasure sells gauze bandages on the side.
Its regular job doesn't pay well. Enough
angels have left positions and found themselves
in need of something to keep Pleasure in
business. Looking up for answers isn't
any more absurd than dancing on the heads
of pins or thinking gauze prevents infection,
is it? Angels would only shake their heads
if asked. Pleasure doesn't really care
about the angels. It doesn't know
for sure if gauze is only a gesture,
or if it does any good. Suffering
often runs a scarred hand over the gauze
on its way home, but never buys any.
Suffering likes to say the gauze costs too much
for what it does. But nothing is hurt,
Suffering says, by just touching it.
And Pleasure likes to tell the angels
how the fevered hand has passed over
the gauze, almost in the form of a blessing.

A Fever of Vertebrae and Opera

The vertebrae are dancing, the boy
keeps saying. The vertebrae
are dancing. His mother cries.
The washcloth on his forehead
has to be returned to the bucket
of ice and water every four minutes.
The fever won't break. The ice
melts. The boy soaks the sheets.

The vertebrae are dancing around
a pole and humming, the boy
says, the sky an opera gone mad.
The libretto, he imagines, raving,
is the sad story of a dance
every vertebra knows by heart.
Each click of bone on bone
is an article of faith. The dance,
the boy whispers, is a prayer.

The mother places a sliver of ice
over the boy's spine near
the small of the back where
the flesh forms a shallow pool.
Someone wearing a mask kills
a king at a dance. The vertebrae
fall around the murdered king,
the sky a wail of violins and brass.

The vertebrae are weeping,
the boy says. His mother
watches the shudder of flesh
cross his back and then return.
The fever is breaking, no ice
left anywhere in the house.

As Memory Collapses, Believe

If water's a language the living speak to the dead,
oscura is the rotted hull of a boat turned over
at the edge of a river. A heron lifts from
the shallows where a splintered oar is a scar
in the water, the grain in the wood visible
in the air gone gray. And no matter what ruin
is rumored, there was pleasure in the wood,
in how the sweat of a palm stained it
with what could almost be called love.

A heron wades downriver from the oar
and the rusted bridge. Ignore the signs
that condemn it. As memory collapses,
believe *oscura* is the family name
of the man who first touched the wood now graying
under the river. Or the tune he hummed
as the oar took form in his hands, which had trembled
in the air condemned by a woman's cold back.
Absence rose from the scent of her flesh
like the oar rises from the drought-lowered water.
Like corn rises, a pale stubble, in fields
wavering in the distance and the heat.

Any story told to explain the lure of water
is titled *Oscura*. It ends with the scar
the flight of a heron leaves in the dry air
that condemns wood and the gray memory of wood
in a river stained by the frenzied stench of heat
and chemicals. It ends with the dead speaking,
in whatever language they died in, to a woman
on a rusted bridge who can mimic the song
of a cardinal, that mad pulse of longing
that burns the air as it flies. *Oscura,*

the woman whispers, her gray eyes
stained by whatever sky scars the field.
It seems to be a warning. And the heron
discovers more than something as dark
and ruined as language in the river.

Whisper *oscura* for the trembling, mute fish.

The Etched Shape of the Heron

I want the present to hear me if I cry out.
Rilke called the deaf angels. For them,
the present is a vague remembrance
of flesh, like ripples in the dark river
long after a heron lifts from the shallows
to name the sky with the rough flourish
of a signature I almost recognize.
As if I've known the trembling hand
that scrawled the letters. Rilke believed in
the possibility we have. I need
a distance between me and the past.
Like what the fish feels in the etched shape
of the heron over the shallow river
a canal was cut beside eighty years ago.
Though since it's late October in the northwest
of Ohio the wind down from Canada
is cold enough the heron is a shock.
Cold enough to question any distance.

If this were the past, I might make the mistake
of turning the heron into an angel.
Such usurption is a thing of the past
only because I want the present to be
my crying out, and a form of grace. I need
a voice that could rise from the things I love
and leave them trembling with its passage.
No matter how much I want angels
to touch the dark waters of this world, nothing
can keep this gray-blue bird from crying out
in a voice that rises from a throat
that knows the way sorrow trembles
in the flesh like some clumsy, tattered fish.

Nothing can let Sead Todorovic forget
how smoke rose from the five men tied to

the burning tire at Omarska. No matter
how much I want to believe
there are angels, those five burning bodies
testify that everything I've touched
is a wound. Tonight, Emin Jakupovic's mouth
is the open wound of his nightmares,
men pale and limp lined up naked in the cold
for him to kneel before and, without prayer,
bite off their testicles for the pleasure
of the guards. The voice risen from
such a wound could name the present
and cry out with enough pain to say
how many ghosts could tap dance on
Emin Jakupovic's teeth, or how many angels
it would take to burn loud enough
to let Sead Todorovic touch his wife
without the smoke leaving ash on her
body, or how any heron can sign the name
of a god whose angels could come to
earth in the burning forms of bodies.

Emin Jakupovic knew the men who forced him
to swallow the testicles of two men before
they'd let him stop to be sick. They laughed
at what came out of his throat, and gave him
a bucket of water and a broom to clean it up.
One had served him cheap beers at a tavern
where men they killed had been regulars.
Behind the bar was an old painting,
a graceful rendition of some large bird
lifting out of an almost frozen body
of water, the hint of steam rising
a halo around the figure of the bird.

Rilke said beauty was only the first touch
of terror. The world he knew is less substantial
than the wader in a painting which is

barely a memory in this place
where the only birds left are scavengers
settled on the bodies of men and women
dumped in the fields. Still, his words touch me
and my flesh trembles with a past
full of deaf and blind angels. This trembling
is what's left of the present. And listening
to the crying out of belief in
any rough signature is a desperate plea
for even the possibility of grace.

The Damage Time Does to Bodies

What they call History
is nothing to vaunt of,

being made, as it is,
by the criminal in us:
goodness is timeless.
—W.H. Auden

We hate knowing everything is waiting.
And no matter what we do, our flesh,
which isn't some tarpaulin draped over
unfinished work, records our two-step
with time. We try to keep track of distances,
but even fog ruins our chance to see things
as they are, or what lies in the distance.
Which isn't a country we can name.
It turns out the Old Masters were wrong.
Things they thought constant have changed,
perspective a trick learned early on.

We make things more and more complex.
And no distance can save us. Not even
the cavernous space under a tent put up
at the edge of town, in which a man claims
to know truth. *The Lord cleansed me and my life*
began anew. A choir sings. A pale woman
rises and struggles to enter the glow
around him, his promise to heal. Touched,
she wants to believe what she knows can't be true.
The singing goes on until morning.
No one is saved. The cancer takes her
just weeks later, his touch the last thought she has

before entering the cold, open country
of memory, where distance has no meaning.

Her name isn't spoken by now. Even
the healer is whole and breathing
only in someone's memory, and not
the sepia photograph a believer hung
over a fireplace where real wood burns. A cliché.
Posed. His large hands on a woman's head,
his eyes up as if to see heaven. We know
he can't see the ruin in her suffering,
or how his own body, carried thirty feet
by the impact of a train, will dance. All this
is in a distance he can't make into a country
his followers can know the name of.

We know. This is about death. How stories
we tell to lift us out of the earth
we have to lie in are lies, and the best
we can come up with. Auden knew. His poem
doesn't end with Icarus' forsaken cry
or the punctuation of the splash,
but with the wake of a ship that couldn't
be bothered to pull a pale, far-fallen boy
from the green water of Brueghel's canvas.
Commerce was calling and it followed, calm,
like decorous grief. The way friends tell us
to get on with life. The dead, they say,
would have wanted it that way. They're wrong.
The dead have nothing to say. They turn from
the living like we turn from them. Like us,
they work to forget loss. Or ignore it.

Like the healer, who forgets the sad people
he touches. Their loss. He hates the time
between towns. His hands tremble, waiting

to burn his voice into poor souls who come
looking for things he'll convince them they've found.
Working, he believes he can heal anyone
who wants to believe in something so much
they'll believe in him. Dust leaps in the harsh light
with his voice. It seems all things are possible.
People kneel for his touch. But a time comes
no one will touch him, disease broken over
his flesh. He sleeps outside towns and lives off
what scraps he can steal. He believes his flesh
has taken on the suffering of those
he touched and promised to heal, so he comes
to a tent where the sick pray to be touched
by a man who can raise their flesh with his voice.
Women scream and hold their children. *Satan,*
a man tells him, *be gone from this holy place.*
He limps off in the role of demon. Outside,
a man pays him two dollars and says to follow
the tent to the next town to earn two more.

They want to cast him and his suffering out.
Town by town, they want him to persuade people
he once touched to believe in another's touch.
The train is atonement for all the pain
unmoved by the false promise of his touch,
his flesh a mystery he almost believes in.
His body dives into a field where men work
hard. They scythe wheat, sheave it and stand it
in shocks to dry. No one sees the body
plummet into wheat they won't reach for days.
Finding it, they'll open soil and place him
to rest with common words they believe in
despite pain. For now, they work and hope
weather will let them finish. Children play
far enough from the body they won't fall
over it. On the train, the engineers argue

what they felt. It's not worth going back.
People in the next town are waiting
for the train to take them where they need to go.

We could tell them the schedules they have faith in
are approximate. At best, they can hope
nothing vital breaks down. Nothing's certain
when matter's involved. Things may keep moving off,
growing colder. Or, if there's enough matter
we can't see, things may fall back and collapse
until heat and pressure we can't imagine
burns all the matter in everything
and explodes to start it again. It depends on
what lies in the distance between the burning
suns like ours that melt wax and nourish wheat.

That kind of time, we like to say, means nothing,
since we can't grasp it. As if everything
were determined by our conception of it.
Things don't care if we come to grips with them.
For all they care, we can say some are touched
by God and can heal the damage time does
to bodies. For all they care, we can gather
in tents to sing and pray and weep, or work
in fields to gather bread. For all they care,
we can carry suffering like sores on our flesh
and call ourselves martyrs. Or write poems,
like Auden did, which say guessing's more fun
than knowing, since then we say how things occur.

So the healer becomes a man whose love
for those who come to him overwhelms him.
One night, leading hymns in a tent, his heart
bursts in the midst of song. The people weep
and fall to the earth in sorrow. A woman
he healed drapes her body over his to warm it.

30

The next day no one waits for the train, crying
in a field for a man who had fixed what was
wrong in their lives. The wheat waits in shocks.
The rain holds off out of respect for their loss.
We could say everything waits for the people
to come to grips with their death, but this is
a fiction we choose to believe in or not.
No matter what we decide, in fiction
things obey the words used to name them. And we say
what lies in the distance between the burning
of suns or of bodies. We say when a heart
can take the world and when it can't. And though
the fictive heart can endure any suffering
we say it can, we can't. We need
tricks that can fool us, and rituals
that let us celebrate the distances
we cross to touch and heal each other.

The Urge to Speak

Come up to me, love,
Out of the river, or I will
Come down to you.
                    —James Wright

We wake with arms numbed by blood held back
by the other's body. We can't embrace,
and the words we use to touch ask one thing
to replace another. For you, distance meant
mountains and snow that never reached you.
For me, distance was sky bored with color
over flat land, or the mist tucked into
scarred fields. Closed in by landscape, people
you grew up with rarely spoke. *Don't waste breath,*
they'd say. The people around me spent evenings
telling stories of things they knew or made up.
Beyond the porchlight, even insects had
the urge to speak. And I wanted to
hear one story that made sense of them all.

Now that blood has returned feeling, the best
I can do is hold you, and not waste breath.
Though the gesture may be all we can manage,
I want to fit your past to mine. It should
be possible. If a thing as tenuous
as moisture in the air reforms landscape
by corrupting light, we should be able to
carve the rock of memory with our flesh.
Love, let's revise our pasts. I want to
tell stories on a porch where hands
tingle evenings from the bloodrush of work.
I want stories to come as my body
settles in to the calm ache of bone and flesh

coming back to a shared idea. The way
people would gather around the porchlight
where insects whose names I invented flung
their brittle bodies in lust and in prayer.
People came to talk of work, and drink
the coffee my mother served that steamed
like the fields on late October mornings.

Love, let me say the dry air you breathed
was a struggle, your lungs scarred by
a childhood illness. Let me say crows
are burnt air, or sooty angels come to
welcome you back from your body. Let me
tell them on the porch how I found you
almost naked under an oak, abandoned
by its shade and burning. How crows cawed
at me. How I touched you back to us
from a past you moved through asleep.
How I helped you off the earth and held you,
careful not to press too hard the flesh
that would fall from your body. For days
I'd find small, translucent pieces of you
in the tub, on sheets, and know it was
nothing to worry about. Just a way
our bodies have, shedding flesh to deny
we're named by what we touch.

Which is another lie. The flesh holds
a memory of what forms it. Despite
any stories told on porches where people
gather to invent the fictions they will
live in, despite mountains with their lie
of snow or the sky with its betrayal
of color, despite the layers we can't
burn off or break through, words planted
by touch take root and grow
a crop we can harvest and live off.

Morning Visitation

This field of March stubble you stand in
near the edge of a depressed Ohio town
is not the horizon, and will burn
in minutes. A boy everyone thinks of
as *slow* will think it a visitation,
and will tell all of us who gather
to watch smoke lift from blackened ground
of how the toes of the angels burned
with a light that set off the earth. *Music*
that was a woman's breath, he'll say,
rose with the flames. You'll put your hands in
your pockets. The woman you would touch
if your hands really could heal anything
won't be with you and the rest of us
on the edge of a charred, smoking field
almost outside of town. She will be
with another man whose hands have healed
her flesh in ways yours can't. And angels could
live in the fog that hasn't lifted yet
on this morning before any story
of fire or music a slow boy heard
as breath. They could be sighing for your hands.
And I could be somewhere behind you,
unable to see your hands tremble
in the translucent air as if they wanted
to form a body from the fog that was
whole. Not until you held them out
almost in a gesture of prayer towards
the vague shape of a stand of trees
as if it were nothing but the body
of a woman you didn't know how
to touch. Perhaps I won't remember
any of this later when I see you

with the rest of us, the awful scent
of burned earth in our lungs. Perhaps
it will be enough that you've suffered
the indignities of this morning's fog.
And the slow boy won't speak of music
or of angels. *The birds,* he'll say.
You should have seen the birds flying
in the ash. How the flames caressed
their frantic bodies and the burning
healed their fragile wings.

Animals Housed in the Pleasure of Flesh

Forgetfulness is useful to the preservation of the individual.
—Paul Eluard

1.

Our breath rose becoming,
with distance, only air,
an elegy written by bodies
which long for touch
the way insects crave
our thick blood. Memory
is air too thin to live on.
Canaries would die breathing it,
their vibrant yellow bodies
giving up on song. Memory
would have music coming
from a car radio clear of static.
She had caught a sleeve
of her linen blouse on a low branch,
the snag a white scar
I smoothed out, an excuse
for touch, her pale flesh
a body of faith that required
more prayer than the breath
my lungs could hold. Memory
would burn that sleeve
into my flesh like a wing,
the snag becoming the white breath
of her naked body, the music
I can't remember. Now,
a woman often sings me

to sleep with Welsh songs,
a foreign music to placate
my heart after sex, to end it
imagining blood getting thinner.
The heart, despite its bravado,
is thick with guilt. After all,
there is blood on its breath.

2.

The grass was a pale gray stain
rooted in a loam the barest of layers
for our bodies. Rock took over
at a shallow depth we thought
we could dig to with our hands.
And below the last million years
of stone men labored.
Our breath rose toward
a scattered light as much the past
as the dust men breathed in
under the earth. When we were
finished, birds crossed over
through what was left of our breath.
They were only grackles,
but their flared boat-tails left
a wake in the dark we were
sure we could follow home.

3.

Hard-shelled black beetles woke
under our wet bodies,
our lungs longing for ellipses
of air. What remains
is the sad taste of blood
where she bit my lip,
her body becoming a light
that makes visible the simple,
elegant figures of animals
housed in the pleasure of flesh.
When my tongue touches the scar,
I wonder where she is.

4.

In Wales, men know the ritual
of looking in rock for what is
needed. They know what breaks
between one word and the next,
having kissed the bodies of men
whose swollen lungs had burst
under the earth. They know memory
needs solid beams of oak
to shore it up. They know the hearts
of birds, held loose, hum in black
fingers. They could break
with the loss of sky. Birds don't
sing the same after the mines.
Even the barest breath of gas
changes them. An old miner
once told me, *The gas reminds them*
what they're singing about.
Maybe air just plays their bodies
like flutes through scarred lungs.
Or maybe the hearing changes,
not the song. Maybe something
rises in the blood of men
coming back to the country of air,
the way nitrogen bubbles form
in the blood of divers who rise
too fast from places where water
won't allow light. Places
where fish burn their own flesh
to find food so they can go on
burning to find food. Maybe
the black dust that burns
men's lungs until breath is a pain
they long to endure
isn't an illness, but a ballad,

their ruined bodies the notes
that score it. Maybe
the black bile they'll cough up
is like the burning part
of a fish that never sees
any light but what it makes.

5.

Flesh, a sign, burns and is not
consumed, pain a flowering
from a layer of ash and soil
that goes deeper than we could
dig to. The past rises
from damp ground. It was rising
the night her pale skin became real.
People speak of burning
moments into memory, as if
a lithograph could be burned
into the landscape, into soil
and down to the rock men carve
tunnels in, burned into the rock
and the air trapped in it
so the last thing a scared man sees
before his lungs expand past
the point of flesh is the form
of two bodies entangled together.
Seeing this, he might think
of his wife. How two nights before
the collapse, he was in her
and she chanted his name. But
this isn't what he thinks of. There
isn't enough oxygen to think
of anything as real as this. Memory,
no matter what we say it is,
or should be, remains personal.
She said all around us the elms
were dying, the hard-edged cells
burning. Even the dead
limbs could hold us, though,
she said. She wanted to
climb into the dying wound
of wood and sleep, held

from the predictable damp grass
in the morning. She said
it would wake the dead memories
in our cells. Why was I afraid
of lying with her among the dead
branches? What would
the morning have been if I had?
Not even the dead can answer,
no matter how precise the words
meant to summon them back
from their own concerns.
The old sacrifices don't work,
and the dead can't tell us
what we'd have to do
to reach them now.

6.

Even air has limits. It can be forced
miles below rock to form
caverns of oxygen, dust flowering
in the currents, lungs dark petals
curved round the one true stamen
of blood which blooms red
only in the country of air.
And air longs to love the body,
to know flesh as more
than a translation from a language
it can't speak. We are proof
air loves, the flowering of blood
around a wound only the body
offering the air a gift. But
air doesn't know the loss
that lies under flesh, a taproot
twisting deep in the body.
And no air can know the lines
drawn in the body's dark
that form memory, which is
more than images of animals
locked in gray and dying
cells, more than any air
could stand. Brought back up
to the light it shines dark
enough to make any soul
collapse, and swear
nothing could be more pure.

7.

We can't go down into the body.
Whatever may be etched,
or burned like soot, on the pale
walls of bone that keep
this illusion of flesh
from caving in, we have to
live in fields our bodies
lie down in. Fields where
the dark forms of grackles
move sharp like sickles over
acres of rape, the yellow
an unreal setting for birds
so black. No, we can't go down
into the body. Not even
for birds so black or yellow
they could save us. Not even
to bring back to the surface
bodies we've touched and whispered
the names of in rooms
where flesh was a kind of light.
These bodies rise, and we can
pretend we've called them, a lie
to comfort us. But the canaries
we dream fling fragile bones
against our warm bodies,
yellow feathers drifting in currents
of sour sleep-breath,
and grackles click bitter histories
in our limbs. When we wake
to find our bodies sore,
our skin almost a pain,
we shouldn't blame blood denied
but the frantic aviary
of our night flesh, the hungry
throats that fly sooty air
over fields we can't lie down in.

8.

Begin with breath rising
into a memory of breath.
A rosary of two wet bodies
moving together in a field,
color drained from flesh and grass.
Imagine birds nearby
small as wrens, the nuances
of grays. Imagine the two
lie still, finally, in the vague
form of love beaten down
in grass. Imagine a car
passes by, the driver unaware
how close he is to a place
where flesh is recovering
from what passion requires,
the rush of blood away
from the brain. Imagine
the windows are down,
on the radio an old Welsh song
about a woman who sold
live mussels and cockles
and died of a fever. Imagine
how that music sounds
to the man and woman coming back
to their bodies in the grass.
Imagine there's no such thing
as memory, that even the past
moves off from us at speeds
we can't calculate. The song
on the radio is one a woman
sings to me in bed. Imagine
breath is a rosary,
each inhalation a bead
to finger as prayer leaves
the flesh. Imagine memory
is an issue of faith.

9.

To believe what happened
happened is to live
in the places flesh forms
and to believe in singing,
whether of birds or the woman
lying next to me in bed.
To believe her breath blesses
my hand inches from her mouth.
I don't mean to wake her.
I mean to go on feeling
her breath on my palm,
to not confuse this woman
with any other woman,
this breath with any other breath.
To keep from using the actual
suffering of any man
or woman for anything less
than what they've become.
I mean to deny nothing.
To let all the dark birds
we ignore punctuate memory,
as if what's remembered
needs a grammar of its own.
I mean to let these awkward
black birds congregate
in yellow fields of rape,
and believe they forgive me
any sin words might make of them.
To believe the music
their hearts would hum
if I held them in this hand
warmed by the breath
of a sleeping woman
would be a Welsh tune

sung by the last miner
left in a collapsed shaft,
the air thinning around him
and in his lungs,
his own heart a bird
on an ashen branch
beginning to sing,
or a hesitant angel bursting,
finally, into psalm,
or just an old wound
that reminds him how the breath
of a woman filled
his body with blood.

10.

My wife murmurs in her sleep.
The words could be another language,
or it could be the distance
they've had to travel
to reach someone still awake
has made them dark birds
with calls that sound like punctuation.
There is no telling the sentences
they end, no way to know
if there's enough air left in my lungs
to call her back from the country
she has gone to. A place
where birds return each year
to elaborate festivals
and papier-maché replicas
that are exact in every detail.
People dance around the dark figures
of what could be mistaken for gods.
Everyone's at the parade,
even the men cradling in
their laps the bags which fill
their collapsed lungs with air.
Women wheel them to the front
of the crowds lining the streets,
and the small yellow birds
their faces have become
open their beaks as if the air
were thick enough to peck
whole chunks off to swallow.
After the parade is over
and the men have been lifted
out of wheelchairs into beds,
after their wives have stripped
them of everything but

their bags of air and straddled
their boney bodies and moved
over them, their open palms
warm on the loose skin
of concave chests, stopping now
and then to listen
to the breathing of the men
they love, after the women
have cleaned themselves
and their husbands with the warmth
of a damp washcloth, after
the women have fallen asleep
carefully beside the damaged bodies
of these men who have spent
their lives under the earth,
the men lie awake in that country
and listen to the reason
the dark birds have returned.
All night the men sip
from their clear bags of air
while the bitter sound
of feathered bodies
entering one another goes on
until the air they breathe
seems thinner than ever
and they fall asleep clutching
the bags to their chests.
When they dream, these men
living in the country
whose native tongue is the murmuring
of my sleeping wife,
they dream of a place where the air
never runs out, where
there's so much sky
even the papier-maché birds
could begin to sing.

To believe in what happened
is to stroke the stiff,
wrinkled chest of a bird-idol
and imagine the song
that comes out of that chest
formed of ripped paper and glue
is the breath of a woman
warm on the open palm I hold
inches from her mouth.
To imagine memory
is such breath, and that
I could place my open mouth
over hers and breathe
a whole country of air
and remembered air where grackles
and wrens and canaries
fly over two bodies held together
by sweat and the faith
they will remember any of this.
A faith that scorches stone
near the delicate lines of animals,
and says the place
their flesh has formed in
the grass will remain.

Local History

This is how it was. You need to know
this happened. No one saw the bridge
collapse. In the distance, a calf lowed,
the sound a confusion of cause and effect,
a legend of grass and the turning
of one thing into another. *Prolactin*
is the desire, after all, to heal
away from one death to another,
and fear, like the sound of a bridge lowing
under your feet, can keep the body dry.
Even *colostrum,* that early collapse
of proteins in what could be fear or
knowledge, can be confused with sound.
And any story of wood rot and metal
corroding under the calm of a slow river
is the need the calf felt, and you have felt,
for the miraculous to happen under our noses.

The way the bridge fell into the river.
No one with a voice was there
to remark how the water whitened
around it like milk, or to yell a plea
that could bridge any two worlds
as distant as the sound of a bridge
falling from air to water
and the low, lost moan of a calf
hungry for milk. Hormones call in
the sanguine body of local history,
and legends of how the bridge flew
too far from the water and lost
something you'd call desire would
turn the calf into a human witness,
the low an absolute certainty. *This*

is how it was, you begin. Once the bridge
was a white burning in a bovine body,
a need to give, and to keep on giving.
That was how it was. How it should be.

Without your need to know. The bridge
corrodes the river. In the right light,
it turns into the color Icarus became
falling, the color that splashed in Daedalus' eyes
like pure milk. This color is the miracle
almost no one saw, not any story
of wax melting into hormones that could make
any man dream of flying. This is how
local history takes you from a place.
No one knows more than the color of the bridge
in the river that can heal any desire.
No one can say what you need to know.
This is how it is. The fish scatter like rust.

Ghosts of Flesh

for Douglas Smith

The water's between the shock of cold
and body temperature. It changes
with each swell. Near you
in the water, a woman leaps
and pulls a man under. They laugh
and embrace, their bodies an issue
of faith you believe in simply
because of what you can see, and what
you know. The form of their bodies
together is an open grave
for memory, which is a ghost
of flesh. You've come to
this eastern ocean for the first
time. What you've brought
can't be buried and left in sand.
You'd like to say the heart is
something to tend to, the way
the man who had entered
the water beneath
the pale hands of a woman
carving a halo over his body
tended to the transparent form
of the dead jellyfish. How
he carried it from the beach
and buried it in sand out of grief
for something so abandoned.
You know the heart can't be carried
to where scrawny grass struggles
in sand to survive the salt. It can't
be pulled from the body by the raw
motion of the earth or the quiet

influence of the moon. The sand
burns with loss. Something
as sacred as any muscle scars
the beach at the edge of dunes
where a sickly grass haloed by wind
tells rumors of a place certain enough
to let something frail as a heart live
in the ghostly form of two bodies
embracing in water. Whatever
ghosts choose to live in or haunt flesh,
you'd like to believe grass can cover
any scar its roots touch. Even
the more and more opaque body
of a medusa. Even whatever
bodies of stone may surround
the heart, caught in the midst of
a dance to praise love, in gestures
that speak of salt rising somewhere
to form a figure of two
bodies turned toward each other.

Any Water Will Do

Think of the body's loneliness.
  —Louise Glück

In the Sonoran desert, a woman
once told me, flowers bloom that remember
the way light smelled before anyone touched.
Before anything had guilt, or a name.
I learned from her touch deserts can blossom
in the names we give ourselves, the landscapes
we're stuck with. Like the Ogallala. *To scatter*
one's own. Later, I heard the story
of an anonymous corpse tended to,
but not buried, in some Southern town. I was
jealous. Of that dark and haunted body,
memory was all that could wither. Light
touches it through the window where it hangs
like a body once put on public display
for everyone's forgiveness. It becomes
a near barren landscape light knows the way
we know a lover. By touch. This flesh,
unclaimed, is a blossoming of stigmata,
the wound become the body. Lovers ask it
to bless them. Old women dream it comes to
their rented rooms and whispers in their ears
of the local lake. The water rises
over the forgotten maps of their bodies.
Hugo said a town needs a river to forgive it.
Any water will do. Sometimes, watching
this woman sleep makes me remember
the story of how a boy found, in the Sonoran
desert, a woman, her bare, raw back pressed
to a saguaro. Her flesh held the curse of
the cactus, red braille. The boy took her body

off the withered tree and forced her stiff limbs
flat. No matter how he touched her, there
was no way she could forgive him,
no way she can forgive me. And the corpse
that hangs, embalmed, like a crucifix
in the dusty attic of a Southern morgue
has no chance of forgiving anyone, of being
forgiven. It can't make me forget any name,
or what drought can do to a naked woman
blossoming on a saguaro, almost
a curse. That the other corpse becomes
what it becomes has more to say
about our use of the dead than the dead.
Outside Tucson, the brittle flower of
the woman's body felt like salvation
to the boy. Years later, I set fire to
every flower a woman had planted and waved
to our neighbors' faces behind curtains
and glass. The woman's corpse
on the hard ground of the desert
didn't come back in the flames
or the pitiful smoke the burning of flowers
formed. Of her naked body,
all I could see were the red pictographs
the cactus left on her as the fire
consumed the garden. And I cursed
memory for how it bumps against us
like a blind trout swimming past our ankles
in water we're sure we've heard the name of,
though we can't for the life of us say it. Asleep
and sweating under sheets that in the right wind
could be ghosts or a kind of surrender,
this woman beside me believes a desert
is all about remembering. She dreams
unscarred saguaros in a landscape of light.
The flowers blossoming on the thick arms

open like mouths. She wants them to tell her
a name she could carve in stone, but they explode
with pollen and cover her with the dust
of seeds. She lies down in the heat and feels
what isn't her body but the past. One
body becomes all bodies in her dream.
The corpse that drifts in attic dust and directs
the lives of people who know the names it has
forgotten. A woman's body stretched out stiff
beside the trembling of a boy in need
of forgiveness. The ash of flowers withered
by drought and burned down to soil. And one
more body. Not a woman floating, her face
kissed by trout in water named for a horse,
but an angel as lonely as any body
made to return to ash. And the light,
which is not a body but touches them all.
I want to touch the light this woman becomes
in her dream. Burdened with the loneliness
of bodies, it sings of desert flowers
without names, how they burned in its presence
once and, forgiven, were not consumed.

In the Amnesia of Passion

Dark birds I didn't know the name of danced
in tepid water. I asked a local woman
with dark skin what the birds were. She told me
the Spanish name, a word like locusts,
like a curse, like nothing I'd use for those birds
that were everywhere, like grackles in Ohio,
the inhuman crack of their voices almost
a blessing from throats that swallow dust
that could be history or an old sorrow
laid out like ash. Their voices might have been
curses, or prayers. Or the voice of a woman
whose throat was a wound of sand. Her hands could
caress distance out of my back and legs
when she could touch me without the brown body
of anyone's despair or rage taking flight.
She often spoke of the house her father filled
with tribal masks whose sour breath clouded
the rooms. At night, their lips spoke demons
she didn't want to find a way into her.

In Austin, where the landscape is spoken
by old voices, I remembered dreaming
a voice for the masks that spoke of her
body. Their breath in those dreams was mine,
moving over her flesh like dust, or sorrow.
But this woman didn't belong any place
in the Southwest. She's a memory.
Not even her voice is real, unless what's uttered
by the carved lips of sleep can be said
to be real. Memory clings to places
like some time-scarred insect. Think of locusts.
Imagine the sporadic leaping of bodies
in dark clouds. The voracious hunger. The curse

of the insect body, the bones a private hell
to burn in. The past is not a place,
or it's a field consumed by insects. The masks,
whose breath stained the plaster of a house
in Ohio, could have been carved by tribes
whose flesh was darkened by living
in Austin before it had that name. Perhaps
the woman who only knew the Spanish name
for brown jays held in her DNA
the elegant gestures of hands over wood
to form images for the voices of gods. Perhaps
she could've taken me to a dark room in some adobe hut
and undressed while tepid water moved
through pipes. Perhaps her hands would have
carved my face into a faint semblance of some god
she might have whispered the name of.
And it might have been the Spanish word
she had used to name the birds. The past
is not a place, unless it's where words
like *perhaps* remember flesh. In the language
of tribes who burned the carved faces
of gods, *perhaps* could be a curse
or a prayer, depending on a gesture of hands.

The only fragments of their language are inked
on clay vessels kept dry in glass cases
in the Southwest, or carved on masks
in a room in Ohio. No one living has heard
the language, but one morning in Austin
a woman in a dream held a tribal mask
and breathed a word I couldn't make out.
Awake, I'd have risen naked to form
an echo of the carved sign in
that forgotten language for *memory*. Instead,
still half-dreaming in a damp shroud,
I listened to local insects chirr themselves

mad at the return of light and thought it
a lamentation for the wounded, dying
body of history, which is not the past,
but the pale flesh of sorrow that won't stay
in the past. No matter what inked symbol
my body echoed in some awkward position
it took in sleep, any voice whispered in
memory is false, a tepid water stain on sheets
that echoes the intricate carved shape of desire,
which the body only forms part of. Perhaps
the matins of the birds whose Spanish name
is more a curse than a prayer could bless
the barren and faceless walls in any state.

Perhaps memory is the body's matins and vespers,
and the faith such prayers require has been carved
in the form of faces and birds. I want to know
the name of the brown jays in a language
no one living can read or speak that was chanted
through the carved lips of masks painted
the colors of dust. A complex hand gesture
made it the name of a bird, and not
the word said to a lover when the body was sore
with distance and needed the slow motion of hands
carving small circles over knotted muscles. Said
with a different gesture, the word which named
the brown jays could mean the moon was a memory,
a stain in the sky where it had been swallowed
by a creature no one had ever seen more of
than its head. Which was worn certain nights
by a woman who'd dance barefoot in warm ashes,
chanting through the mask, and choose a man
she led into the desert to a cave
where she carved his body in passion and left
scripture in the scars to serve as memory
to everyone who read his flesh. Neither

would remember what had happened in the cave,
which had a name. *Dark where the body*
wakens, or, closer, *Womb of forgetting.*
Any translation is a voice in memory,
or a stain on sheets, the faint aurora
left behind by the pleasure of bodies.

A forgotten language still clings, like the shell
of some short-lived insect, to the walls of caves
in the desert outside Austin, where lovers
have touched words they didn't recognize
with their naked flesh, and the fading memories
of hands pressed to bodies have responded
in kind to the chants left in the amnesia
of passion. Old men have come with lanterns
to copy the words. Huddled in their worn bodies,
they've known, in some way the body has of knowing,
what's been done in those scorched and sacred places,
and in whose names. Perhaps the woman
who named the birds with what could have been
a curse or a god might have led me
to one of those caves in the desert and touched
my body in the old way. Perhaps it wouldn't have
taken scars, but just a willingness to remember,
and a faith in the prayer the body knows
as sorrow to name what needs to be
named in a language we speak, not knowing
the words. Back in Ohio, I think of
the brown jays. How one morning I fed one
missing a leg, amazed at how it clung
fierce along an iron fence and hopped
the red, baked tiles after torn bread. How
it could beat the others to the ragged bits.
And the memory of that bird comes to me
like a blessing, like the touch of a pale hand
on a body older than it was, speaking

a language older than the forgotten tongue
in caves outside Austin. The language the body,
always memory, is carved of, and carves.

The Inevitable Beauty of Gravity

The river here is dirty. No one's willing
to say its name out loud. Boys whisper it
into the warm, delicate ears of girls
they mean to change the color of. The skin
of locals can carry a syllable or two.
Like the local the drunks call Hymn.
A bittern by the river one Sunday went mad.
The violence of its beak wrote almost
the whole name of the river in his neck.
It lost a letter or two in healing. After that,
his solos in church stopped. Everyone
said they missed his voice. Some nights
the scar sings when he's had enough to drink
in a dark bar with a woman's name.
River lullabies of herons that weep
over a man fly-fishing, the Ohio sky
a gray complaint. Sometimes it hums
Vivaldi or Mozart. Next to the river,
erosion's a doubt no faith erases. There,
sleep follows the music of a landscape
cut by water, the color of wheat
a flame against the ash of storm skies.

Naming anything invites confusion. Hymn
drives, the windows down, a road that curves
with the river. Light can glare and leave
retina angels whose wings make his throat
hurt. A heron carves its long shadow into
the road, a hieroglyph he can't read,
the blue body hovering in a current
of air. He thinks, *Music is always about
loss.* He knows it's a lie. He believes
if he spoke the heron would cry out, its voice

bitter enough to convince a man fishing
the shallows of the dirty river that love is
something the skin whispers wet. The river
sleeps through this sad Ohio town. Once,
the moon a pale fugue for violins, a woman
drove Hymn to the river, parked on the bridge
named for a local dead musician and touched
his ragged neck. It started to rain,
the car a symphony of breath and water,
the inevitable beauty of gravity. Neither
would ever name the music they heard there.

Now, Hymn dreams the dirty river
in his body. The scar sings her pale hands.
One night, Hymn drinks the scar
into a frenzied aria in the one bar left
in town. No one's drunk enough yet
to recognize Vivaldi, the tempo all wrong.
Hymn tells the men who drink themselves
into what could be mistaken for pain
that nothing will open their hearts. *Sinkholes.*
All the surveys in the world, he says, *wrong.*
To build anywhere water's been is a risk.
The scar is singing under dirty water.
No one can say where they've heard the tune
that carves through them. Nothing but soil
that remembers hands. Or what's left
of figures carved from sandstone with faith
in another world. What the filthy river has
worn from them is pain. These stone ghosts
don't belong here. They belong to a time
when the neck of a boy scarred by some bird gone mad
could sing in tongues. When rivers could carry our lives
and not be dirty. *They don't belong here,*
Hymn shouts over his scar, going crazy
with a music no one could ever be

drunk enough to name. The worn stone figures
taunt Hymn with old chants, his scarred neck
a distance from the men who shout his name
and laugh in this bar, a curse
made of the river's name. The scar
makes even the dirty water forget music.
Gods don't sing out of flesh anymore.

.

Scars and Faith in Waking

In homes near the center of town,
men have faith in the scarred promises
of religion, and every night
suffer their wives' sleep. Water surges
in the calm air above the fountain
of a goddess sculpted in the pale arms
of her husband, Death. The rumor of
the spray drifts over them and cools
their dream flesh. Wolves roam the edge of
town, starved and sounding like jealousy.
All day, Indians sit on rusted chains
and smoke in front of the used car lot,
whispering to the gray and black wolves.

The gray stone cut out of local mountains
to build the courthouse is being cleaned,
sandblasted by men with masks
who curse the pain in their lungs despite
the cloth. Indians avoid the viscous dust.
The wolves are hungrier, and come
further in to town. Men who work late shifts
breathe the dust in their sleep. In Waking,
no one believes the wolves are any more
dangerous than the dark tinge on the stone.

The stain is as clear a sign as they are
likely to get that ruin has a name,
and a husband, but not her husband's name.
And if the wolves are a reminder
of what they've lost, the dust that flies off
the stone is evidence that even in Waking
faith is all in the pitch. The goddess
comes to everyone except the Indians

in dreams. They watch her sell used cars
at noon, promises made over relics
drifting along the form of her body
like a rumor of dust dreaming it's water.

Or water dreaming it's dust. Waking,
the Indians might say, is built over
sacred ground, the used car lot at night
covered by the souls of ancestors
in the jealous guise of wolves. Slashed tires
found in the mornings are pictographs,
voices of the dead that speak of the curse
that follows living. In town, children
draw stick figures over the tracks of wolves
who seem to dance to some aberrant waltz.

And scars heal exactly how scars heal
in any town. The carved fountain attracts
nondescript birds people feed without
thinking, the water permission to care
for everything. When a car passes,
the birds rise from the pavement, a sleep
disturbed by the hunger of motion,
jealousy dusting the air with what could be
echoes of a waltz played too much
in the fashion of a dirge. The Indians
recognize the tune as an old one,
and hum it to soothe the wolves' despair.

With such music suffering the air
it's easy to feel abandoned, to imagine
the goddess is a real woman
who used to live in Waking but left
years ago to visit a darkened country
where the mountains aren't gray and speak
a different tongue. When she didn't

return, the town council commissioned
a local Indian artist to carve her
out of native stone. It was his
idea to make her Persephone,
Hades the scarred body of a man
whose chest was once opened by wolves.

The dust, jealous of the stone, leaves
a veil the goddess wears everywhere
water's too cursed to reach. The story of
the statue's a lie. Everyone knows it.
The woman whose form it remembers
is the sculptor's wife. The rumor is
he caught her one afternoon with
the man whose arms now confine her
in stone, a man whose name was
a mournful howl out of the mountains
no one could imitate. Every scar
that marks any body adds to the dust
the goddess hums under, to the sore
music scored by children in dirt.

Or to the lies the Indians know
are lies that everyone believes.
Like the wolves. To begin with,
there've been no wolves in Waking
for almost sixty years. And yet
there are the tracks, and the music
men make out of the breath of women
asleep. A music something moves to,
furtively, among the pine trees
that shade all the roads out of town.
And everyone believes it's wolves
the Indians whisper to, not something
as mundane as memory. The stain
is a sign, they say. They don't know

what's coming, but they believe it
isn't just the dust carved off stone.

No one knows what the Indians believe.
Some mornings, one of the old ones
washes the windows of the showroom
on the used car lot. If you stand
at just the right distance, you'll see in
the dark glass a reflection, not his
but a cross between a man and a wolf.
It will be an illusion, a trick
of the light, but for that moment
you'll believe even the goddess is
possible. You will believe even a man,
covered in dust and carved out of stone
can hold a woman in Waking,
with enough passion to heal them both,
and long enough to become a god.